The Soul Already Knows

Judith S. Royle

The Soul Already Knows

Copyright © 2017 by Judith Royle

All rights reserved.

No part of this book may be reproduced in any form or by any electronic or mechanical means including information storage and retrieval systems, without permission in writing from the author. The only exception is by a reviewer, who may quote short excerpts in a review.

Book design by Judith Royle

Tom Bird Retreats, Inc.

Redesign: Colleen@clcconsults.com

This is a Non-fiction Memoir

Written by Judith Royle

Visit my websites at www.judithroyle.com

and www.soulgenesis.com

Printed in the United States of America

First Printing: 2018

Published by: Tom Bird Retreats, Inc.

Paperback ISBN: 978-1-62747-390-3

Ebook ISBN: 978-1-62747-340-8

Dedicated to Chardonnay,
my esteemed travel companion,
navigator and fur baby.
I am blessed with her unconditional love.

Table of Contents

Foreword vii

Chapter 1	Is This All There Is? 1	
Chapter 2	And I Signed Up For This. . . 4	
Chapter 3	A Star Is Born. 9	
Chapter 4	We Are One. 14	
Chapter 5	The Olive Branch 21	
Chapter 6	Lessons Learned 27	
Chapter 7	Soul Contracts 29	
Chapter 8	Power Becomes Empowerment. 36	
Chapter 9	A Choice To Die On A Hill. 45	
Chapter 10	Curiosity Killed The Cat. . . 49	
Chapter 11	A Product Of Humble Beginnings 58	
Chapter 12	What is Love? 68	
Chapter 13	Let There Be Light. 84	

Foreword

As a lifelong friend and more recently a student of Judith's, our paths have ebbed and flowed throughout the years. Judith's first career took her into the field of education, whereas mine in communications. We have traveled together, shared many laughs and shed a few tears along the way. Our common thread has always been a shared curiosity about life and a mutual respect. It is with great pleasure to see the culmination of Judith's journey turn into this book. Judith turned out to be a true communicator far beyond just words. When Judith asked me to write the foreword to her book, there was only one possible answer and since you are reading this, I said yes!

Judith's book, *The Soul Already Knows,* takes the reader along her personal journey humbly and with a sprinkle of humor. The book is for anyone who is curious or searching for answers perhaps not yet defined in their minds about how to make the best of this lifetime. Each of the thirteen chapters unfolds a life's lesson brought into perspective from Judith's own journey. The lessons are captured in the chapter titles, quotes, and reflections that summarize key truths as an aid to tie it all together and fit into the big picture. The spiritual and life lessons from her past, present, and future lives are a gift to us.

The book speaks of God and the reader is encouraged to replace the word with whatever belief that resonates with them personally. The universal lessons transcend and apply to all spiritual life.

Let Judith's stories and parables draw you into the powerful lessons such as how to purposefully take control, learn from the past, and break patterns that might limit you from your highest potential. Einstein has been quoted as saying, "Insanity is doing the same thing over again and expecting different results". Stop the insanity and it starts right here by reading on. What helps break these patterns is conscious awareness (Chapter 10).

Another lesson described is facing a fear or any limitation and why it has been given power. Judith says, "Our own reality is only our perception and that can change depending on whose eyes are doing the seeing." This book teaches readers to open their eyes and heart to life's possibilities.

The focus on family and family relationships is another tenet. We don't get to choose our family members, but we do get to choose how we allow them to impact our lives. We also can choose a family of like mind as an alternative to ensure a supportive and positive community.

One of the simple actions to jumpstart change is to list five things you are grateful for in the morning and again the last thing at night. This can work like magic. I tried it and it truly helped focus on what is important. (Chapter 12).

The first step is reading Judith's book, which will help the reader to become aware of unconscious beliefs and actions. The second step is reflecting on Judith's life lessons and how they can be applied to open up life possibilities. But I am getting ahead of myself; just keep reading and discover for yourself.

Judith's book reaffirms it is possible to understand why we do and act certain ways and there is a vibrational match for everything, with unfulfilled contracts that might need attention.

Travels through this lifetime can draw upon the learning from this book. It takes a spiritual guide and healing practitioner to write this kind of book that connects life's lessons, brings it life through storytelling, and makes the lessons accessible for all. Judith's stories come from a place of deep and personal honesty. Judith never sugarcoats her life's hard lessons, so others can benefit from her journey.

As I read through the chapters of this book, I focused on the book's journey. Each time I read the book, the journey expanded, and I took away different learnings. I encourage you as the reader to pick this book up over and over and each time the takeaways will resonate differently and blossom. Enjoy

Judith's book and most importantly, enjoy and take control of your own life's journey.

Jani Yates
CEO Ad Standards,
Toronto, Ontario, October 2018

1
Is This All There Is?

Let us forget the frustrations of the past and think of our unfulfilled potential.

-- Thomas P. O'Neill

There is a cool breeze across my back, but the sun soon warms the places on my body exposed to the elements. I can feel the blades of grass tickle my toes even though I am wearing well-worn sandals. From down the hill a short way comes the sound of bleating. My companion is busy at work ensuring the sheep are herded and there are no strays he must chase after. I love to daydream here on the hill at my station. A fleeting vision crosses my mind, reminding me of the noise and clamor of family life in the little town at the foot of the hill in the valley. Such unhappiness and cross words are spoken without any thought as to how hurtful they might be. Words trip across their lips effortlessly, creating drama sure to poison one's inner sense of beingness. It is with a heavy heart that I ready myself to start down the hill to bear the weight of such sadness and spitefulness that will greet me at the door. I much prefer to be alone with my staff, sheep, and shaggy companion.

The air is fresh and clean, clear of toxins that are waiting to invade my sense of peace. Surely there must be something better, more loving and harmonious out there. I'm not even sure what those words mean since I have never experienced them. I see it in the sheep I tend, their tenderness shown between mother and little ones. My dog encompasses the pride of having a duty well executed and is there at my beck and call. Unconditional loyalty and respect are given freely. So, yes, I guess I do know those feelings as they relate to my animal kingdom.

I see in the distance an imaginary world of love, respect, peace, harmony, and joy. There is a longing deep within me for these things. I feel like I am bleeding from the inside out and the only way this condition can be healed is through love. Then I ask myself, "What is this word 'love'? What does it mean? How does it feel to give it and receive?" There must be a Being who can show me the way.

Usually I am the shepherd, but I need to be led to that place where I will find lovingness of a sheep and its master. Who will show me the way? I yearn for this to fill a void of something that is missing in the core of my being. Ah, the sweet smell of the grass and the songs of the birds. These will have to suffice until I find what I am seeking.

I hear a rasping forceful voice from down the hill. I have spent too much time in my reverie and will pay dearly, as my mother awaits impatiently for me to find my way home from my day's work. It is really my day of respite from the festering hatred waiting to fuel the fire of human disillusionment.

2
And I Signed Up For This

"We all have different desires and needs, but if we don't discover what we want from ourselves and what we stand for, we will live passively and unfulfilled."

—Bill Watterson

I remember, as a soul yet to become part of the physical world, the excitement and anticipation of my prospective new life. I envisioned a world of blissful joy. When I had been conceived, I listened from the womb for signs of this world I so desperately sought. I listened for the words, the tone of voice, and the feeling behind the words. I listened, quietly waiting for any rays of hope that I had chosen the family just right for me. As I took in the essence of my surroundings and the prospective family members that were slated to be a part of my world, a tsunami of disappointment washed over me. This must be an error; the Beings who directed my soul to this womb must have been mistaken. I called out beseechingly, "Please take me back, this is not what I agreed to, please take me back. I did not agree to this."

A benevolent voice responded, *"Oh, but yes you did. You wanted to discover in your own way what love is, by not being loved. It is your contract. This is your life's lesson and that discovery will be your gift and in turn you may share with others. You will receive many gifts as pearls of wisdom not many will have the honor of receiving. Go forth into the world and be willing to receive and above all be willing to serve.*

This theme of living light and healing is a thread woven in the tapestry of your many lives each connected and giving insights and learnings for the next incarnation. To thine own self be true. Be ready, willing, and deserving of the many talents and gifts you are given, for they are not given thoughtlessly. Use them with integrity and a loving heart and be the first to forgive and forget. This is a tall order for you in human form, but your higher self knows and remembers. You just need to listen for you already have all the answers within and are written in our Akashic Records. All you need to do to is access wisdom with an open heart and mind to the answers within the Records. And you will see, feel, sense, and remember. The soul always knows."

With a heavy heart, I bided my time until the midwife appeared with her entourage of assistants. I had forgotten the birth process and how frightening it was, so I closed my eyes and felt the muscles around me contract with the screams of a banshee. If I could have stayed inside that warm cocoon I surely would have. My destiny path had begun and there was no turning back. My father had a weathered face with close-set eyes. I looked into them and they stared back empty, lacking character and strength that I was wanting to see. He seemed pleased that I was a boy. At least I would be useful in tending the sheep. The midwife was the most caring in how she tended to my needs. She offered me as a bundled newborn to my mother, but she turned her head the other way. Another child is the last thing she needed or wanted.

Only seconds born into this strange world and already I could see my future. My quest for unconditional love had begun and a bumpy, dusty, winding road it will be. I steeled myself for the journey ahead. I hoped and begged for help and assistance for the road ahead. I wonder if The One knew of my plight. At present I am beginning to believe I have been abandoned and everyone around cared only for themselves and what feathered their nest. A sorry beginning to what I had hoped to be a beautiful enchanted life.

The days, months and years passed; life unfurled into one hostile argument after another. Many threats among parents and siblings abounded. At times I stood my ground and declared this inhumanity expressed toward each other was not among the teachings of The One. I was met with a cold calloused hand across my face or a stony silence. In my alienation from others, it became easier to keep my silence. The group mentality presided, however, as it was much easier and served their purpose to create a box in which to file my oddness.

They apologetically explained to others, "He is a little odd, in his own little world, not like the others." These words were said within earshot, so my "strangeness" was reaffirmed on a daily basis. Their words didn't bother me as, I had my own world in the beauty of nature and the animals within it. They were my family and so I learned early on about Spiritual Family and that they don't have to be blood related. The answers came from deep within from a place of remembrance of the Ancient Ones and the Ascended Masters. I dreamt of meeting the Anointed One.

3
A Star Is Born

"The opportunity to orbit the Earth, witnessing multiple sunrises and sunsets every day, looking back to our small blue life-sustaining jewel from a distance, gives me the greatest sense of anticipation."

—Sarah Brightman

There were whispers in the town square where the women gathered at the well to share in the gossip of the day. There were lowered voices, but I listened carefully and gathered as much information as my invisible-like presence could gather. Over the years the whispering was incessant; there was a promise of the coming of a prophet. The anticipation was mounting, and I waited patiently.

We were blessed with a clear night, calm breezes, and the road well-lit from the light of the stars overhead. We wondered if we would be walking for the remainder of the night. We had no notion of distance, as we had never travelled beyond the hill for tending the sheep and the village down below. We climbed a steep rise and paused at the top to catch our breath and benefit from a sip of water at a nearby babbling brook. With our thirst quenched, we assembled to continue our journey. One of my fellow shepherds pointed at the twinkling lights below. We wondered if this is where the star would lead us. We quickened our pace in excitement hopeful our search would soon reveal the outcome of our discovery. We could hear the lowing of cattle in the distance and the odd bark from a dog chastising a member of the herd ahead.

We began our descent into the village ahead with nervous anticipation. We approached the gates of the town and were allowed entry. Our senses began to identify the sights and sounds of a village alive with activity even though it was well into the night. The sound of the donkey's hooves echoed off the walls of the buildings and the space felt limiting and claustrophobic. We ambled down narrow alleyways searching for something; we knew not what. Finally, we spotted a structure ahead worn with time and weather. Through the uneven boards of the shed appeared a shimmering light. Immediately we knew we had arrived at our desired location, humble as it seemed. The door was slightly ajar, so we advanced cautiously, hoping we wouldn't disturb what was transpiring inside. There were three men waiting outside with us, but they were nothing like us. They were dressed in fine linens and seemed confident in their demeanor. They were each carrying a gift of some kind. It hadn't occurred to us that we should have brought gifts to honor this event. With that, a young man came to the door and invited us in.

At once we were stunned with the brilliance of a golden white light. It was a different kind of light than that cast by a candle. It was iridescent and shimmering, alive with a resonance of something unique and precious. There in front of us was a disheveled young woman looking tired and spent, but smiling with pride and amazement. She was holding a newborn child whom emanated this golden white light. His skin was aglow, and a shimmering halo appeared above his head. We were speechless and could think only of kneeling by his bedside to offer our prayers of gratitude for being included in this event. Our lives would be changed from this moment on. This moment would be etched in our hearts forever. We moved aside to allow the other three brethren to see the majesty of this event in time never to be repeated.

As we gathered our thoughts outside the building, we decided to begin our return to our village. We pledged to each other to keep our participation and attendance a secret because we knew intrinsically some would not be pleased with the birth of this child, named Jeshua. And so Jeshua's life on earth began and I knew our paths would eventually cross again.

As I paused to reflect this visit to a past life, I wondered could that just be my imagination? I decided that was of no importance, for what I needed to do was ascertain what I learned from this snippet of time over 2,000 years ago. Immediately the phrase, "Ask and you shall receive, it will be given," popped into my mind. I asked the question, "What did I ask for?" My thoughts flew back to my youth on the hillside, while tending my sheep. I remembered thinking, there must be more to this life. I questioned "Where is the light of the human heart?" All I could see for all those years was darkness, resentment, frustration, guilt, shame, and rage. I had been blessed in being present in the birth of the One, Spirit. I now knew what that loving light looked and felt like.

After basking in that golden Creator substance, I realized there was no turning back. For every lifetime after this one I would have that beautiful Godspark of light imbedded within me. There will never be excuses about not knowing what I didn't know. There was a knowingness that was instilled in me forever more.

4
We Are One

"We each have a sixth sense that is attuned to the oneness dimension in life, providing a means for us to guide our lives in accord with our ideas."

—Henry Reed

The years passed and I continued to live my life as I always had, but certainly more mindful of how I treated others. My belief was to treat others as I would like to be treated. This was a philosophy devoid of flowery words and promises of hellfire if one didn't measure up. To me, there was no benefit in complicating a straight forward, simple way of life. The voice in my head reminded me to do and be my best at all times. I did not learn this from my family or townsfolk. I learned it from the light of the Chosen One.

I am now too old to tend to my sheep; I have passed this down to my sons and they now have the privilege of sitting in the sun thinking their thoughts about humanity. I ask myself, will they ever think the thoughts I once did and reach out to find the meaning of life? Sometimes I walk along that same road reminiscing about following that bright star in the sky. Now, my spine is curved and my footsteps are more measured. I use my staff to give me leverage and balance. I will continue to walk until my limbs can no longer carry my weight. Life has been good, and I have been truly blessed.

This day the sun is shining brightly, and it is warm. I can feel a trickle of sweat run down the full length of my spine, but I continue my walk, not knowing exactly what is compelling me to continue on such a warm day. My head is bowed, and I am concentrating on putting one foot in front of the other. I sometimes think my feet lift higher than they actually do and find myself tripping over the smallest pebbles. Last week my friend tripped and fell and broke his hip. It is highly unlikely he will ever walk again, and I know he will lose his lust for life if he loses his freedom to walk where he feels inclined to go.

Sheppard's do not thrive on confinement, rather it dims the light of our souls' beacon. I have watched my dear brothers lose their independence slowly and surreptitiously to the younger folk. They have no patience with us as they can't know what it is like to walk in our shoes. And so, I concentrate on placing each foot where it should go and proceed regardless of the aching in all my joints.

I pause to take a deep breath and I notice a figure off in the distance walking towards me. It will be nice to meet a traveler and to wish him well wherever the road takes him. As he nears, I notice he is tall and young, walking as if he had purpose in his life. I see a glow around him and it looks faintly familiar. I steady my gaze to get a better look but the glow becomes even brighter as he nears. The golden glow is warm and welcoming. I am pleased that this stranger will be friendly. Some youth prey upon old men like me because we cannot defend ourselves. He was almost in front of me when

I recognized the light. I approached him and drew close to his body. He was mildly amused, but accepting. I reached out my hand and said, "I know you, you are Jesus, the Christed One." He nodded and smiled benevolently.

"That I am," he replied. "You know of me?"

"But of course, I was there at your birth, I answered. I have always wanted to be you." He answered, "But you are me and I am you."

I had never seen such a miraculous golden substance in the light. That is how I knew, it was a different light radiating from another dimension.

We sat down by the side of the road under a shade tree and Jesus began the story of his life and his current direction. I was mesmerized by his voice and his piercing eyes. I focused on each word he uttered, these were pearls of wisdom. After what seemed an indeterminable amount of time, he shifted his sitting position and started to rise. I followed him and as we began to walk it didn't seem to matter that I was walking in the opposite direction from where

I began. There were several moments of silence and then Jesus began to speak.

He told of his search for disciples who would carry on his work after he was gone. I inquired as to where he was going. His answer was vague, and I decided not to pursue the topic and walked in silence. After several minutes, he turned to me and asked if I would be a fisher of men. I didn't know what he meant so I asked him to explain. He told of his search to find those who would continue his teachings of Love. I told him I didn't know much about love and I wouldn't be suitable to carry his word. I was too old and gnarly to keep up with the others and my family would need me to provide for them. He nodded knowingly and smiled; and I wondered what he was thinking.

Later I would regret the answer I gave him and I knew fear was what kept me from joining him. Who was I to deserve such an honor and how would I ever measure up to him and his disciples? I am just a lowly shepherd. And that belief stayed with me many lifetimes after that and kept me from living my life purpose, my destiny. I never thought I was good enough to amount to much except what my family did for generation after generation. It was just what all sons of their fathers did.

Jesus' words reverberated in the core essence of my being, "Live by my teachings in all ways. Know the Beatitudes. Be a fisher of people as I have taught you. Do not judge others, especially yourself. Always look for the good in others as they mirror the good in you. Realize you can't be all things to all people. Be what you teach, in this way, you can never go wrong. *As I am so are you.*"

As I look back over the many past lives, this limitation persisted and was behind the demise of every dream I had. In fact, I believed that dreams were just dreams. They were wishes that didn't come true, they were part of a fantasy world conjured up to make life more palatable. I have decided that I would seize every opportunity to build a life of service to others. My actions would be based on what was in my heart to live my best possible life. Facing the fear around making decisions would require me to take an action which was a notion I hadn't considered. Perhaps one of my lessons in this lifetime was to figure that out.

As an aging man, I hardly recognized the gift the Chosen One had given me. I could only feel I could not meet his expectations. I was left only to entertain tending my flocks. It was all I was meant to be.

5
The Olive Branch

"We are not held back by the love we didn't receive in the past, but by the love we're not extending in the present."

—Marianne Williamson

That was not the last time I would cross paths with the Chosen One; the last two occasions would be etched in my memory for eternity. I had walked into the village to visit an old friend. I was about to leave and start my trek to my own village, but I heard Jesus was dining with his disciples and the woman called Mary Magdalene. I had desperately wanted to see HIM again since our meeting on the road some years ago. I hid behind a partition, hoping to catch a glimpse of him and his followers. My wish to remain invisible was hopeless; suddenly all the movement and the noise of amiable chatter and the clinking of utensils stopped abruptly. I had been spotted. Jesus called out and bade me to join them. I stepped out from behind the curtain and was stunned to see the beauty of Mary Magdalene sitting to his left. She, too, was surrounded by golden white light.

Jesus rose from his chair, walked around the long table and approached me with an olive branch in his hand. He said, "Offering an olive branch works much better. Keep thinking peaceful thoughts and remember the light that resides in you. Confronting those who are mean and cruel, always remember the light that resides in you."

"Now say, "I am love and light."

With that, the olive branch turned into gold.

I saw him for one final time shortly thereafter. I heard screams and shouting and a loud wailing. It sounded like a death march. I ventured out to the side of the road trying to catch a glimpse of what was transpiring.

There were many others pushing me out of their way, but a young lad elbowed them and motioned for me to stand with him. Without words he assured me that he would protect me. I wondered what could be causing such a stir and then I saw a broken man dragging a cross on his back with a crown of thorns on his head.

There were threads of blood trickling down his face and his skin was ashen. He seemed oblivious to the throngs of chanting people surrounding him. He faltered, lost his footing and fell on the hard, roughly hewn cobblestones only to be whipped by one of the Roman soldiers pressing him to move faster.

My stomach heaved and I found myself in an alleyway relieving myself of my last meal. I couldn't take in what I had just seen, it seemed so barbaric. I had seen him not so long ago enjoying the food and company of his colleagues and cohorts.

Surely this must be a nightmare; it couldn't possibly be truly what I thought I saw. I turned around again to make sure my eyes had not conjured up a scene from another world. I could see his back laced with streaks of red, which marked the whip's territory. I heard the noise of the heavy wooden cross as it chafed against each cobblestone on the road. Each clunk sounded like a last breath taken. I couldn't bear to watch what ensued; I could only guess, as the custom was to nail criminals or those who dared to challenge those in authority to a cross and let them die a slow painful death.

Instead I went to the garden of Gethsemane and waited. I prayed for his death to be swift and painless and for those others that were his constant companions.

How distraught they must be. I relaxed into the recesses of my mind to transcend these feelings of pain, shame, and guilt. I had always stood on the fringes of Jesus' ministrations to the people like a moth to a flame. I was afraid to stand in his light, sure that eventually those who ruled would take him down for fear of the power of his words and the effect they had on people. Maybe if I could have risen above my fear, my allegiance may have changed this outcome.

That experience found its way into the many lives after that. Every time shame or guilt expressed themselves, those feelings were exacerbated and triggered by that ghoulish scene. The weight of the guilt became a burden overriding all other emotions in any subsequent lifetime. I seemed doomed at the outset in my pursuit of happiness. This fact gave me pause to think about what could be done about it now. As the thought crossed my mind, HE appeared in a translucent form, a defined form yet mystical in nature. He bade me to sit with him for a while in my garden.

This was a beautiful garden I had created at one end of the property which was shaped like a figure eight. In the middle where the lines crossed there was an arbor which housed flowering vines. A statue of an archangel sat on a cement pedestal situated in a spot where the sun shone a brilliant column of light as it rose in the mornings. Jesus bade me to sit on the bench in front of the arbor and when I sat beside him, he embraced me in a loving hug designed to melt all less- than-positive feelings away. He assured me that guilt was a waste of energy and urged me to let it go, it can serve no purpose. He instructed me to focus on lessons learned and how I would incorporate those lessons in daily life. I wondered why

I didn't listen to him and take his words to heart, instead of continuing to hold on to my belief that I was not worthy of his love. In fact my life had unfolded into a series of heartbreaks; one after another, betrayed by every significant other in my life. I believed God, the Father had abandoned me and I did not deserve any better. I marveled in disbelief that the Chosen One loved me enough to visit me to allay my fears and give me a new lease on my life. It is like the old adage, one can't see the forest for the trees.

6
Lessons Learned

"Some of the best lessons we ever learn are learned from past mistakes. The error of the past is the wisdom and success of the future."

—Dale Turner

Three days after the crucifixion, I went to his tomb to leave a gift for the messages he shared with me over the span of his lifetime. When I arrived, the stone barring the entrance to the cave was rolled away from the opening and upon inspection there was no body on the stone slab. I was confused and didn't know what to think. Had someone stolen his body? Surely not, sanctions for such a deed were steep. I left it to another mystery in my life and decided to start my trek back to my home village.

Tired and distraught, I focused on shuffling one foot in front of the other and eventually my mind found its sanctuary in fantasy. In my reverie, I heard footsteps behind me, I turned to see who it was and there was my Lord and Master. I stopped long enough for him to catch up to me. I looked at him in disbelief wondering of what service I could be to him. Again, he instructed me to take heed of several instructions I must follow and complete.

Know the Beatitudes and infuse them into your daily life. Always speak your truth and be your authentic self.
Love yourself as you love me.

"These things you know for sure; do not be deterred or stray from the truth," he said "Know the most important relationship is with God, the second is with yourself and then others. Relationships must stay in that order."

He asked me how lessons from previous lives or the impact of events in past lives have affected certain outcomes in this life time. I replied there too many to count.

7
Soul Contracts

"If you look to your past or even your present to see why you are here or what your purpose is, you may get stuck in a limited view of yourself. Instead, look beyond your years here on earth, reconnect with the divine, and bring forth your soul's legacy into the present moment."

—Debbie Ford

Over time I came to understand there is a vibrational match for everything and that is what attracts certain people into my life. There are the unfulfilled contracts that have needed attention, too. A husband has appeared in several lifetimes and always had the same purpose.

A past life takes me to a cabaret where I function as the owner and dancer. I am older and don't dance very often since arthritis has settled into my joints. My knees and hips are particularly painful. I limp among the side streets, cane in hand, to the Chinese side of town. It is my life line. My significant other and I never did marry because I had no time for family life and my time and energy were focused on my business. We had a life together of sorts, a co-existence, so to speak. He frequented the club and took great interest in the younger versions of me. He could be very solicitous if there was something in it for him. He took great interest in those who had the large doe eyes, with no apparent friends or family in life. I commended him on his kind heart and generosity as he went out of his way to see them home after a riotous evening of dance and frivolity. It was all I could do to sit at the bar and observe my patrons and keep some order and decorum with a few who knew little about gentlemen's manners.

I was an institution, respected for who I was and my ethics in business. It was just part of the evening to step in between two young muscled men as they began to fight over who was going to experience the delights of a lady beckoning with the lusciousness of her bosom. Pierce, my companion, was no match for the young lads, but he had his own methods of magnetizing these women still dreaming about the life they wanted to create. He never gave me pause to wonder if he had ulterior motives. He was quiet and unobtrusive and asked for little in compensation from me. He was just there, and I trusted him with the finances of running the business. He was in and out of an evening and was busy investing profits in collaboration with other high rollers. It was his public persona and no one questioned him or his motivations.

I started doubting his integrity when I was passing by the door of the dancers' dressing room. The door was slightly ajar, and I overheard him requesting the presence of one of the young dancers. My beauty had started to fade, and I was conscious of the threatening presence of the younger nubile dancers. While I was shocked and displeased with what I saw and heard, the pain in my knees rose above my displeasure. I had planned that after my saloon closed I would visit China Town to find relief in the opiates they had to offer.

In fact my mind constantly roamed to my personal cubicle where I could find an escape from my waning enthusiasm for life. It was my only source of relief and I had come to depend on the sense of euphoria that crept through my body as I experienced its effect. While enjoying the soothing effects of the drug, my mind was free to wander and create new scenarios of me rejuvenated into a new kind of life. I could plainly see my life in a small town away from the hustle and bustle of this large city. I am sitting on the porch of my tiny cottage steeped in my energy and faded beauty. I see myself as I sit and watch my flowers grow in my abundant garden, happy to know this is all I want and need. There is such a yearning for this life I so richly deserve that I conspired to plan a strategy that would give my loving mate his just desserts.

The first thing I did was prevent him from having any access to monies collected every evening by announcing a plan for my retirement. I decided it was high time I looked after the bookkeeping and to close the establishment in stages. His face turned ashen with that announcement and I knew there was more than wandering with the young girls afoot.

As I familiarized myself with the financial side of the business it became clear that profits were being distributed elsewhere. My guess was the profits were to feather the lifestyle to which he become accustomed. I found myself wondering why that hadn't occurred to me before, never doubting his integrity. He had become a master of deception so that no one knew of his secret life. I blamed myself for my stupidity in overlooking his actions. Rage filled me, fueled by years of pain to have maintained the life to which he was accustomed.

Over the years I had made some interesting friendships, ones that facilitated a thriving business and furthered my status and credibility in the community. I decided it was time to call on a long-time friend for counsel on further action to be taken. Extreme care needed to be taken, as Pierce had the keys to my accumulated riches. I left it in the capable hands of my friend who knew exactly what had to be done and it would be better for me to be unaware of the burgeoning plan of retribution. One evening Pierce's face was absent among the sea of patrons and I knew he had disappeared never to seen again. Interesting how no one asked of his whereabouts and nobody seemed to care. Such was the impact of his selfish life.

I stayed true to my dream and envisioned that enchanted cottage in my dreams and waking hours. It was so clear and real to me; I could even smell the pungent aroma of the stargazer lilies as they bloomed in the flower bed in front of the porch.

Jesus' voice filtered through my reverie, *"Stand in your light embracing all aspects of yourself. You are a Human Being with a shadow self as well. To be whole you must accept all aspects of yourself. Anchor yourself in the light and do not waver. It is not possible to dance in and out of it and be consistent. Make the commitment and do it. I am the One and you are me. What I do you have it in you to do as well. Be a fisher of people and be of service to humanity. Always take care of your heart first; then others, for you cannot tend to others when you are broken."*

I became a mentor to many of the young women of this small town, seeking to see more of their identity than being someone's daughter, sister, or wife. This was an oddity since most were a reflection of the family and environment. Maybe some of them held glimmers of hope to be all their potential said they could be. Yes, it was fulfilling to be a mentor to such young prodigies; it was a sense of accomplishment that my life did mean something. I asked myself the question, "So Dear Heart, when you die, what will be your legacy?" The first and only thing that came to mind was, to be known as a wise loving woman.

8
Power Becomes Empowerment

"Power can be taken, but not given. The process of the taking is empowerment in itself."

—Gloria Steinem

One lifetime was not enough to teach me the lesson of empowerment. Another lifetime was needed to teach the importance of taking my power back to create my own reality. This one in particular regarded power of the husband over the wife. This lifetime was in the age of pioneers. My husband and I lived in a small log cabin in the woods. The road to town was not far off but far enough away that nobody dropped by to visit or much cared about either of us, for that matter. He was cruel and often projected his unhappiness on me and inflicted a black eye or a push down the steps. There was no love lost between us, but my hands were tied and I had no way of setting myself free.

I was helpless and hopeless, imprisoned in a life of a slave living in a log cabin with dirt floors. I cooked in a huge pot over a fire. I had become quite adept at creatively making meals with the same root vegetables, utilizing spices I could beg, borrow or steal. Nothing was good enough for him. He constantly complained and in a rage one night he threw the stew I had nursed all day over the fire at me. Gravy and morsels of meat and vegetables dripped off my apron and hem of my dress. I looked at the dirt floor and I thought how nice it would be to have wooden planks as a floor, so I could actually sweep it.

This is the life I have chosen, but I found myself wishing for something else. Maybe there is a seed planted deep within me that is telling me I deserve more in life. But then again, how would I know what to ask for if I had only known this? And yet the seed had been planted and all I needed to do was water it with the same attention afforded to the food I grew outside in my garden and in cooking the meals. I said nothing, but inside my head, a switch flicked to the "ON" position. Somewhere in the depth of despair, I decided I had reached my limit. I decided to focus on my long-forgotten spiritual body, for it needed to be nurtured and bloom, too. To blossom into a fragrant flower and be all things to me as my higher self. Despite my circumstances, I will grow into the best version of myself, emanating all that is wise from The Ancient Ones. And there I sat staring at the dirt floor wondering who was I to wish for such a thing? But still…. I began to plan; tomorrow the plan would be implemented. Again, my husband announced his presence with the crashing of the wooden door against the wall. Some things I could count on as the sun rose and set every day, and this was one of them. I moved quickly out of the way to protect my bruised and broken body. His physical size was daunting and he used his physicality to dominate all things.

I often wondered what made him such an angry man. Is he a walking imprint of his father and how was he a role model for that beautiful child his parents brought into the world? Did his mother hide in the corner out of fear too? He would never speak of it and finally I stopped caring. But I do wonder what unfinished business I have in this life with this man. Maybe it's to find a freedom I have never had. A plan began to germinate and to all intents and purposes nothing changed except for the fact that I was more pleasant than usual, oddly enough.

Life continued on its normal course and no one was any wiser. Burt from the Apothecary in town was a lovely man, had a soft spot for this shadow of a woman and unwittingly assisted me with the plan. This plan evolved from the seed that I deserved better. My husband's rages sucked the energy as a vampire would. During one of those episodes I stared at the back of his bulbous head as it shook to the rhythm of his pounding fist. He grabbed the first thing he saw on the shelf and hurled it across the room. It was a small mason jar with a few sprigs of Queen Ann's Lace. As I watched, detached from the scene, I thought it symbolized his lack of respect for the beauty in life. It smashed into pieces and the water from the jar formed a puddle of mud on the floor. A stream of blasphemy burst from his mouth as he berated me again. He knows that if he keeps me skittering across the floor and distracted with fear, he maintains his stronghold of domination in this life of misery he has created for us both. I stealthily hid my body behind the partition that separated the bedroom from the rest of this woe-begotten bundle of sticks called a house. His voice boomed across the dense air, "You stupid bitch, I should never have expected someone worthy of me from a mail-order bride company. You should be kissing the ground I walk on. If it weren't for me you wouldn't have a roof over your head and you would have died of starvation long ago. Weak as a mouse you are, and ungrateful at that!"

I had heard this tirade a thousand times before and told myself many times that the words can't hurt me, only his fists do. I had convinced myself that whatever he said, the words would fall on deaf ears, yet I knew that my soul was withering and dying a slow death. A fleeting thought caused me to wonder what it would be like when he died a slow death.

Yes, Burt helped me acquire the arsenic for the job of dealing with those pesky rats nesting in the hide-outs of this domain. As one week blended into another, my husband's health began to fail for no apparent reason. He became lethargic and found he needed to take frequent naps.

He didn't even have the energy to raise his fist to me, which pleased me greatly. He took our only horse to see the doctor in town, but the doctor couldn't find the root cause of his lethargy. I watched closely and observed the dimming of the flicker of life force of his black heart. For the first time I saw a glimmer of fear in his eyes. It was as if he knew there was something awry, but couldn't quite put his finger on it. He had lost his capacity for rage and withdrew into the dark corridors of his mind.

I turned my back and my routine continued with my daily ministrations of cooking the meals for the day. While my back was turned, he was unaware of the slight upward curve of my lips. I was patient; I had years of practice. He began missing his afternoon chores, lacking the necessary energy required for fence-mending and instead chose to rest on the daybed by the hearth. He constantly complained of cramping in his belly. Finally he became bedridden and could hardly look after his personal hygiene needs. One evening I took my lamp over to his bedside to check and see if the end was near. He motioned me to lean over so he could whisper in my ear. Since he was so weak I no longer feared he would take that opportunity to use the back of his hand and leave a red imprint on my face.

Instead, he looked at my in a haunting, regretful way. He professed a sincere and genuine, at least in his mind, apology for the years of abuse he had inflicted upon me.

I responded by nodding as if I understood his need to absolve himself from any guilt or shame as he prepared for his transition to the other side. He passed away in the night, alone. I found him in the morning in the same position as I had left him.

Immediately I pulled my suitcases down from the shelf and began packing, folding everything meticulously. When I finished, I sat down for a cup of tea. I thought of all my sewing and designer skills that I hadn't used in a long while and decided it wouldn't take long to refresh my gifts and talents. With that. I gathered my things, balanced the load on the cart, tied the horse to the cart and took hold of the reins. I trotted off down the road with everything I owned in the world and didn't look back once.

Reflection:

One might wonder how many contracts need to be negotiated before lessons are learned. The patterns that have emerged are fairly consistent. My significant other men seem to have little respect for me. They are engaging in the beginning, but once a commitment is made, the rules change and the focus shifts to how his life can be enhanced at my expense.

Is this an Eternal Pattern of Peace where I need to create drama to find the peace in my world? Or perhaps the pattern is destruction where whatever I build, I must take apart only to rebuild anew.

In examining past paradigms, it may be that to understand what love is, I need experience what it feels like to be unloved. Do I believe I am unlovable? An underlying pattern is the strength I had against all odds. No matter what the circumstances, I landed on my feet. My realization needed to be that I deserved and should expect much better than what I was getting in these lifetimes. Has the notion that male superiority is an accepted fact a generational miasm? As long as these belief systems are activated and running, I am doomed to these kinds of relationships and my archetype will remain that of the Amazon Woman. If my perspective were to change in this present lifetime, my behavior and priorities would shift as well. Time spent on healing my world view, teaching me deservability, worthiness, self-esteem, and self-love would certainly create inroads to healthy relationships. If I focused on the strengths, worked on the areas of challenge and demonstrated gratitude for even the challenges and the gifts they bring, the Universal Law of Attraction would swing into action. God's plan is for me to receive all the best the Universe has to offer, but there has to be an energy vibrational match for that to occur.

9
A Choice To Die On A Hill

"You've got to pick your battles, Pen, but then fight to the death for the ones that matter."

—Tiffany Schmidt

I spent several lifetimes as a strong male warrior incapable of asking for help. In fact, to ask for help was seen as a weakness. I was slain in battles in several lifetimes. Many times of being speared by opponents' sabers created hips that couldn't move properly. Broken kneecaps from falling off horses were all hazards of my life. I was often the commander and led my troops into war fearing nothing and no one. Fear was not part of my vocabulary.

On the final day of my life, I woke to the smell of wood fires as the young lads designated to look after the needs of their fellow soldiers bustled about preparing for the day ahead. I hoped my plan to cross the river a mile below where my enemy's camp was located would be successful. I knew we were outnumbered and I would have to rely on my wit and strategic mind to win this battle. The side I was on had been losing battles for the last three months and the king was getting ready to cut his losses and discontinue sending soldiers to replenish their ranks.

Winning meant crossing the river and accessing the cliff, availing the horses hooves to create traction in the muddy slope.

The mist was rising off the water and provided the camouflage we needed. There would be no wild guttural screams from the ranks as we approached our target. Success depended on our ability to be stealthy and make no sound above a whisper. We gathered to get at our appointed space beside the river. A few hours earlier I had sent one of the young lads ahead to watch the enemy's camp, to see if there was any sign of their knowledge my clan was waiting to spring into action. From a mile away, I observed the complete ignorance of the enemy's presence. Perhaps we had a chance. What the lad didn't realize was that he was being watched, but was allowed to return to our camp followed by a spy from the enemy camp. Our location was no longer a secret and our fate was clearly etched among the clouds in the sky.

I rallied the men and led them across the water in the mist and we reached the other side. Rising out of the rippling water, we began our ascent up the hill. As I led my men up the hill, I was greeted by a line of soldiers waiting for us patiently. In a cruel twist of fate, in less than an hour, even though mortally wounded, I saw my whole army massacred; mutilated bodies scattered over the landscape. From a small hill, I surveyed the final battle with my horse standing beside me waiting for a command. It never came, as I died on that hill.

As a person who has lived all these lives, one of my favorite expressions has been, "Is this a hill I really want to die on?" At an unconscious level I was asking, did I really want to confront the issue at hand? Was it possible that confrontation to me meant going to war? During that lifetime, any kind of problems with knees and hips were to be ignored. Real men don't whine and snivel. Even my female companions were unable to help me because of my belief that to ask for help meant weakness. For my warrior in this lifetime there are many situations for me to understand that it is not only permissible, but essential for survival, to reach out for help. Confrontation and standing one's ground does not need to be the Holy War of Roses. There is a way to resolve issues trusting that all parties may find a way to meet our needs.

10
Curiosity Killed The Cat

"All real education is the architecture of the soul."

—William Bennett

In several lives, I was living a monastic life set in the Middle Ages. One life was set on a stage of intrigue and scandal. I stood in the doorway of my small cabin in the woods and smelled the new morning dew and the black soil under my feet. Today was a beautiful sunny day and perfect for gathering herbs and flowers to create my healing potions. I gathered my things in a basket, careful to put on my cloak with the hood to protect my skin from the sun.

I made my way down the path, keeping a razor-sharp eye for plants and specially identified trees. My heart felt wild and free with a deep connection to the spirit of life, Mother Earth. I gave thanks as I made my way down the path and prayed for a plentiful harvest. I thought I would try a new part of the woods, one that I had scanned a few days ago. I remembered hearing the trampling thunder of hooves as the city's guards rushed past me; they were following orders to arrest the young medicine woman who was suspected of consorting with the devil. I hid behind a tree, but not soon enough. My pregnant body was not as quick as it usually was and one of the horsemen caught the edge of my cloak out of the corner of his eye. He reined in his horse in front of me and as the horse stamped with impatience, he asked what I was doing in the forest so far away from town. I had to identify myself as the recluse from the cabin off the beaten track, an answer that piqued his interest. He took in my graceful stature and beauty despite my swollen belly and apparently noted in the back of his mind he would seek out my bed in a few months.

I was well aware of his admiring gaze as I had often experienced it with men of all ages. It was my inner beauty, though that was the real attraction. It emanated as a mystical light that surrounded my countenance. He cautioned me against dallying in the woods because one never knew what situation might challenge my safety. I nodded thankfully and returned to my search for the contents to fill my basket.

The townsfolk knew of me and my healing abilities and sought me out in the village market I frequented weekly. I tended to infections, broken limbs, and bouts of flu that swept through the town. I had saved many a life and was carefully watched by the men who tended to the King and the royal court. They envied my abilities and reputation and they searched for reasons to have me arrested as they curried favor with the upper class. My ability to heal with my special concoctions of herbs I collected in the woods further fanned the flames of jealousy; a crusade to be rid of me ensued. The whispers of the court finally found the ears of those with influence and power.

One autumn evening, after spending the day creating my potions, I sat on my front porch rocking my chair taking stock of the awe-inspiring life I lived. I had few friends, many acquaintances and my loving cat, Patches who was curled up in my lap purring loudly. Suddenly I felt the vibration of my chair on the porch floor and heard that familiar sound of the pounding of horses' hooves. I felt a sense of impending dread as I watched the group advance toward me. The men's faces were carved into frowns of intended purpose. In a cloud of dust they stopped abruptly, with one of the horsemen jumping unceremoniously off his mount. In one giant step he was on the porch with his gnarled hand grasping my upper arm. I didn't even have the chance of protesting as he flung me across the horse, and tethered me to the saddle. What would become of my baby resting in her cradle inside my hut? I must persuade these men to let me go back to get my child. None of them listened to me.

As we arrived on the bridge to the town, I could hear the townsfolk gathering in the square, apparently wondering what could be of such interest at this time of day.

Mother Superior soon realized it was me who was going to provide the entertainment.

I was dumped on the ground and I felt the sand from the street gritting in my teeth. A group of nuns walked quickly past to the Mother Superior standing in the darkness of the corner of a building, I knew this woman! She dispatched her young lad helper to go to my cabin and retrieve my baby while she concocted a plan to save me. She told the King's representative that I was about to be embraced by the church as a novice nun. The plan was quite brilliant because the law stated that the church superseded the law. So I was saved by the Sisters' embrace and I became a nun to avoid being stoned to death. My child was sent to a convent far way where no one would be privy to the knowledge of the biological mother except for the Mother Superior.

Along with the loss of my child, I wondered as I took this escape route was this to become another prison of a slow death of my free will and choice? But I soon rose in the ranks, as a Mother Superior, I made it my business to secure donations from wealthy patrons ensuring us a livelihood and care until our death. The priesthood ruled the church with an iron fist and amassed fortunes carefully hidden. We were not only ostracized by that priesthood, but our male colleagues seethed with jealousy. We flaunted our wealth by decorating the walls of the church with priceless artifacts demonstrating our importance and high position to the world. I was deft in the measures I took to hide our coffers from my greedy peers. I was a force to be reckoned with, skeptical of the Cardinal's political affiliations and endeavored to out-maneuver my male counterparts. Such was my spiritual life within the parameters of a rigid self-gratifying religion. Significant others from these lifetimes emerged in the present lifetime to either resolve conflicts, assist with my present path, or learn other lessons with me, as they did many lifetimes ago.

Reflection:

Now how does that fit into the big picture?

The core wounds of betrayal and abandonment are interwoven throughout these lifetimes and is one of the reasons why we remember past lives: in each life it is our quest to heal those wounds, like peeling away the layers of an onion. With our soul's origination, we saw ourselves as separate from God and these core wounds are part of our soul right from the beginning of its inception. We have inflicted these wounds on ourselves and are carrying that vibrational frequency to attract those who will do that service for us, that is, to betray and abandon. Other core wounds that we may carry are isolation, invisibility, injustice, struggle, victimhood, and displacement. It is only by taking personal "response-ability" that we heal the results of self-defeating contracts. A core wound is like a calling card.

"Hello, my name is _____, let me turn around so you have a better shot at stabbing me in the back."

That's a bit of an exaggeration, but that's the vibration I carried and put out into the Universe.

Each of our souls is unique in our own way with one of a possible ten Eternal Patterns that drives our behavior. It's like the drive in a gear shift, so even though we may not be aware of our Eternal Pattern it still sets the stage as to how we adapt to life's trials and tribulations. Each of the patterns are affiliated with a chakra and is described as to how we respond under stress.

In the case of my precious soul who has lived many lives, my eternal pattern is Curiosity. How that manifests in daily life is that I have to know how things work, the "whys" and the "what fors". My language would sound like, "If I could just get my head around that I could understand." There is a strong desire and need to know what makes things tick. Fortunately, this is one of the easiest patterns because I am a "bottom line" kind of person. "What do I need to do to get this done?"

What helps break these patterns is conscious awareness. Once I realized how all the pieces fit together in my soul profile, I could endeavor to make decisions as to how I was going to change those vibrational frequencies and attract healthier relationships. That also pertains to letting go of toxic, unhealthy affiliations. This may mean severing relationships with certain family members, especially if there is a history of physical or emotional abuse. For some there is a belief system that defies letting go of family relationships: "Well, it's family. You have to overlook that if it's family." It is fairly safe to say that no one in the family will show you respect unless you respect yourself. It is all part of free will and choice. Focus on family, but try to create a family of like mind who is an interdependent community. We just need to remember that we have to own the choices we make and not point a finger at someone else as causing our hardship. That is placing yourself in a position of victim, and a victim never learns from their experience because they are always blaming someone else.

Reflection:

Once again Jesus' words were heard as subtle as a warm summer breeze,

"Although it is laudable to help others, you must always see to your life and nurture relationships that foster the potential in you. True vulnerability isn't to be confused with weakness. Being open to others is a strength and should not be underestimated. Authentic embodiment is a process often learned later in life since so often our identity is tied up in how we define ourselves, whether that's through being someone's daughter, son, wife, husband, father, mother, or career."

11
A Product Of Humble Beginnings

"Trust yourself. Create the kind of self that you will be happy to live with all your life. Make the most of yourself by fanning the tiny, inner sparks of possibility into flames of achievement."

—*Golda Meir*

Reflection:

We can only do our best with whatever skills we have. Our soul's journey depends on the eternal pattern of curiosity that binds us to the quest of our best possible selves. Rather than judging another for their unique qualities and making assumptions about the path they have chosen, seek to be compassionate for every soul's road to discovery. Just because a group decides something is true doesn't necessarily make it so. Take a look at how our cultural mores have shifted over the centuries. Some belief systems that were once believed to be true never were true, are not true now and never will be true. Even the way in which we adapt to challenges may have been viable in the past, but we are now having to learn to follow our instincts in consultation with the mind. Our own reality is only our perception and that can change, depending on whose eyes are doing the seeing.

Guiding my cart over the rocky terrain was taking its toll on the durability and life span of my cart and certainly on my back. I wasn't getting any younger, and I wasn't sure how many more years I had left visiting from village to village preaching the word. My thoughts bounced around in my head in tandem with the jerky movement of the wheels hitting the boulder-strewn dusty road. I looked forward to reaching my next stopover and setting up my booth at the local tavern. It was noisy and raucous but all the sheep of my flock could be found there and it saved me from travelling from family to family as I spread the word of a living God.

I could also continue to imbibe from the huge barrel of red wine I carried in the back of my cart. It is a wonder it hadn't either bounced or rolled off its resting place. I was looking forward to sitting on a stationary chair and gulping down my first taste of wine for the day. Listening to the townsfolk tales of woe may come later, after my thirst had been satiated. I peered ahead in the blinding sun, thinking the town was around the next bend. I could hear the faint voices of the townsfolk as they went about their daily tasks. The drawbridge was open, which pleased me greatly. I didn't have to cajole the guards or share my wine to get in.

As I passed the stone arch I heard a guardsman call out, "Who goes there?"

"It is only the travelling friar here to spread the good word," I replied.

"Oh ho, friar are you sober or have you been finding your way stone drunk?" he bantered.

THE SOUL ALREADY KNOWS

At the risk of provoking the guardsman my face remained impassive and I replied by saying, "No my son."

With a clear way across the bridge I proceeded down the main street looking for my favorite tavern. I slid off the seat, carefully waiting for my feet to land on the solid stable ground and I could breathe a sigh of relief. This town will be home for the next month until my work here is complete. The tavern owner came out to greet me; after all, I was a good customer and the tavern owner's wife fed him, so it was a good pact they had. Rather than drive patrons away, I drew in the townsfolk because I listened to their problems and after a few slurps of wine I was pretty entertaining myself. I never could hold my spirits of the wet kind.

As the sun set, the ranks filed in after a day of hard labor in the fields, anxious to relax and release the pain in their backs felt after years and years of the same work, day in and day out. They called out to the barkeeper for the mead they had been waiting for all day to relieve them of their thirst. The hilarity of bawdy jokes, singing limericks and dancing on tabletops was the order of the night and I heartily joined in. I awoke with my head partially submerged in the horses' water trough. Thank the good Lord someone had been kind enough to prop my unconscious head on the edge of the trough, literally saving me from drowning.

At this point I was only drowning in my own wine. For the remainder of my stay, I must be more cognizant of my station in life at the seminary and remember I must put a more substantial moral foot forward. A voice in the back of my head whispered that it was too late for that. Well, I wasn't getting any younger and old habits die hard. This was my life and I was doing the best I could with what I had.

Although I hated himself for doing it, I found myself in a reverie of my early childhood living with my mother as wild animals would. My mother had been raped by one of the guardsmen and she was left with an unborn child and no roof over her head, She had no way of feeding herself, let alone another mouth to feed. She foraged for food in the forest, eking out every edible morsel, sleeping in caves or a naturally formed lean-to or deserted shack. It became increasingly difficult for her to retain her agility and lightness of feet as her belly grew in size. At least she was physically strong and could bear the extra weight she was carrying. It was a miracle she eventually carried me to term. She had stolen a piece of material from the town market so she could at least swaddle me when I did come into the world.

When the time came she found a secluded spot beside a spring-fed creek. When the pain began she could feel the warm wetness of her water breaking. She sat back on her heels and moved with the rhythm of the waves of pain, careful to make as little noise as possible. She could not risk being discovered for she would surely be arrested, and they would take her baby away. With a whooshing sound, it was over, she had me, a beautiful baby boy. She chewed off the umbilical cord and tied it in a knot, swaddled me in the safely guarded pieces of fabric. As quickly as possible she cleaned herself as well as she could. She must now find a safe haven in which to rest and regain her strength and tend to this new life.

For the first six years of my life, I learned impeccable survival skills from my mother. How to hunt, forage for plant life, and build inconspicuous fires with damp sticks. I was an avid learner and my mother was proud of my innate intelligence. She knew it would save my life one day.

As we gathered edible mushrooms one afternoon, we were accosted by a band of thieves. We could tell by how they were dressed and their manner of speech. One of them jumped off his horse and lunged after my mother. During the scuffle my mother was holding her own against her attacker. This was met by much guffawing and sneering. Taking pity on his cohort losing ground, one of them threw a knife toward my mother's attacker and he grasped it by the hilt.

With one motion of his free arm the attacker slit my mother's throat in front of my eyes hiding behind a tree. She bled out quickly and in the space of minutes, I had gone from being carefree with my loving mother to an orphan with nowhere to go. They heard me crying, felt a surge of conscience and one of them picked me up by the arm and slung me over his saddle. The leader informed the others they would take me to the monk's monastery where they would provide a home for me. And that was the beginning of a whole new life for me. My destiny called for me to shift to a new direction that would change the trajectory of my life. There are expectations that certain things happen as a matter of course, like the changing of the seasons. For me, my message was, "Open yourself enough to release your expectations of how things transpire. You don't know what you don't know so get out of your own way. Leave it up to the Divine Spirit who can show you what is possible and it can be beyond your wildest dreams. Align yourself with others whom you admire and respect, thus raising your vibration to meet theirs. Never sink to a lower level out of pity or the desire to fix the life of someone who needs to follow their own path."

As I grew into a man, I blended into the life of the montesary well. I knew enough to follow the rules, acquire the habits and routines, and know my place in the pecking order of religious life. I grieved the loss of my mother in my own way unable to speak of her to anyone else. I was handed over to the brothers with the story that I was found wandering in the forest unaware of where I was and where I was going. They presented themselves as good Samaritans as they went out of their way to give me a safe haven.

In my adult years, I decided it was time to visit the outside world to share what I learned from the monks. By travelling from town to town sharing the good word, I could regain the independence I once had as a child and enjoy the penchant for wine I learned from my Brothers. It was all I knew and this lifestyle enabled me to use the talents I had acquired. And so, I lived my life doing my best to uplift and inspire others.

Reflection:

Not everyone is suited to be a Deepak Chopra or Oprah Winfrey, nor is it necessary to live our lives believing we need to be famous if our lives are to mean something. The simplest service to others is just as important as those who are widely known for their work. It is the intention behind what you do and the way in which you execute your purpose that determines the quality of the life you have chosen and co-created. How we do one thing is how we do everything. If you don't keep a promise you have made to yourself, you will break promises you made to others. Living a life based on karma and retribution is missing the point; it takes the focus away from our soul's purpose. Choose three words that are non-negotiable and live your life according to the importance and the meaning those words have for you. The choice of words is unique to your set of values and by living the truth of those words, you can actually be free rather than imprisoned.

12
What is Love?

"I've learned that fear limits you and your vision. It serves as blinders to what may be just a few steps down the road for you. The journey is valuable, but believing in your talents, your abilities, and your self-worth can empower you to walk down an even brighter path. Transforming fear into freedom - how great is that?"

—Soledad O'Brien

Reflection:

It is a commonly used expression, "The school of life, here on earth," but there is also a school of life on the other side. Of course, that makes perfect sense in that if there weren't learning experiences, one lifetime after another would look like a revolving door and each life would be cycles of life lesson repetitions. God had a divine blueprint that we are all one and created to be perfect in His image. But, we asked, "What if we are separate????" Ask and you shall receive, and so we received with our souls' origination the polarity of good and bad, black and white, masculine and feminine. The journey of finding wholeness lies in healing our core wounds and learning lessons the Universe provides for us. The process is like peeling away the layers of an onion. Even an onion has a central core and we also have the ability to be whole, to ascend and join the Enlightened Ones.

As I opened my eyes, I saw swirling curtains of colorful mist. I was confused as I looked down at my feet and saw there was nothing. I looked around trying to focus my eyes in the foggy mist and I thought I saw the outline of several forms. There was nothing distinct about these forms, in fact, there was nothing tangible to them. I wondered where I could be and with that I heard the word, "Welcome!" It wasn't something

I actually heard; rather it was more like a thought pattern that crossed my mind. And then a "knowing" occurred where I realized I was my higher self. I had met my highest and best possible version of myself through meditation in the third dimension, but had never experienced a convergence of all aspects of my soul with my heart and mind. Now I was pure heart without the need to think. I was the pure form of love and I felt another worldly ecstatic bliss.

It was time to reconcile the life from which I had transitioned and prepare for the training I would receive to begin a new life of new lessons carefully designed to lead me on the continuing journey of wholeness. What unfinished business did I have from the previous life that I will address in the next life? That will become my destiny or fate. How I chose to learn those lessons is my free will and choice. With the assistance of those souls who travelled this path before me, I will conceive my life map of the lessons yet to be learned. But for now I have received my new purpose on the other side of the veil as a spirit guide.

In reviewing my previous life, I had a different perspective from this side and resolution of conflicts in intimate relationships did not always achieve a satisfactory outcome. In fact, resolution took the form of revenge, the shadow side. There were several lifetimes, not just the last, where my paradigm to discover love was to know what it was to be unloved. From my perspective on this side I thought it was a cruel, harsh way to discover what love is, but effective nevertheless. With this past life I discovered what love was and changed my paradigm to a new blueprint. I am love and loveable and attract only those who embrace this ability and are emotionally available to give and receive what life is really all about, the coherence between the mind and the heart in a heart-based reality. That is the contract for the next lifetime, but in preparation for that premise lies my purpose to be a spirit guide to those who are currently on the same road of revenge for the betrayal of perceived loved one. I must redirect my new charges toward that road of forgiveness not just for others but for myself.

I wait to be called upon for guidance and direction, as I wonder what beautiful soul will call out to me for encouragement and support.

There she is, sitting on her back deck sipping her fourth glass of red wine. Her name is Sarah. She is thinking and puzzled by a long-standing lack of communication with her husband. He has always been a man of few words, but there is something not right and she just can't put her finger on it. I can see it plainly for her, but then I have access to her Akashic Records, so I can see her past and present and also her husband's. I can see the writing on the wall and I have my work cut out for me.

Her thoughts are foggy due to the numbing aspect of the wine. In her mind it is doing the job, but this is not a routine habit she wants to repeat daily. I will wait until morning, when she is meditating, and I will plant a couple of seeds that she may want to plant and water.

Frank and Sarah had just returned from a weekend visit with her in-laws, a two-hour drive away. Upon their arrival Frank's sister had arranged a little get-together to catch up on news and reconnect. Frank had always been teased about Sarah being his third wife. This time a family friend said, "Well, at least this time you got it right." His response was different this time; with a snarl, he said, "Yeah right!" That comment raised a few eyebrows, but nothing was said. But it rankled in the back of Sarah's mind and she decided to address it when they returned home.

The next night she asked him to come to the kitchen to talk. He obliged grudgingly. Sarah approached the topic with unusual calm and proceeded to outline three huge issues that should have been resolved in the early days of their marriage but hadn't. When they got around to the subject of money, Frank accused Sarah of mismanaging money and that was why they weren't able to pay their bills. Sarah had heard this before and couldn't understand where the money was going. Sarah had grown up in a family who walked the talk of the male being the provider. Frank was an accountant, so Sarah had handed over her finances to Frank without question, trusting him implicitly.

As her spirit guide, I suggested to her that was her first mistake and so Sarah began taking responsibility for her own financial stability. For the past three months she had been living on the proceeds of her business, which included her own personal expenses and the food she put on the table. She didn't withdraw any money from their joint account and yet there was a constant drain on the account and it wasn't going to pay the bills. There was something more to this story and she was going to find out.

The first stop was the office of the bank manager. Sarah had known her for years and they had a warm, friendly relationship as well as a professional association. As she closed the door behind her, sat in the chair on the other side of the manager's desk, the bank manager said, "Well, I was wondering how long it would take you to come and see me. That man has been mismanaging your money for 16 years and I think you had better see a lawyer." Sarah's jaw dropped to the floor along with her stomach. She thought she was going to throw up right there in the bank and she broke out into a cold sweat. While she appreciated the manager's honesty she was not expecting such directness. Sarah didn't know where to start, but the manager was prepared with answers.

Two weeks later she sat in the lawyer's office in a black business suit and white blouse with the ties carefully tied in a bow at her throat. The lawyer began, "So where the fuck is the money?" Again, Sarah's face turned crimson as she spoke in a barely audible voice, "I am told I am spending the money, but I have discovered I am not. I have been using the money I have earned through my business and haven't touched our joint account." Without missing a beat the lawyer passed a card across his desk with the name and number of a private investigator.

When Sarah arrived home she wondered if she should follow through on hiring the investigator since she could barely eke out what she needed to live on. Fortunately, she had been hired as a freelance consultant, so she had money her husband was unaware of. As her spirit guide. it took a bit of ingenuity and synchronicity on my side of the veil to lay the foundation of Sarah knowing the whole truth. All the facts involved there were impinging on her quality of life. Here on the other side, us guides, were desperately trying to point out to her that in her work as a healer, she would have to make sweeping changes for her to be in integrity. Spirit was not giving her anything she couldn't handle, but I knew that she must do it.

So Sarah made an appointment with the private investigator and met with him to see what she needed to do. Since Sarah and her husband had a joint account, the bank was able to trace where money had been withdrawn. Frank had not taken this into account because he wasn't using a credit card or writing cheques. Whatever he was doing he was using cash. That was the key to unravelling the mystery as to how the money was draining away. There were two, sometimes three withdrawals per week at the same ATM that was at the establishment of a strip club. What exactly was he doing every evening at this strip club? Sarah was puzzled as to when Frank was doing this because he was home at the same time every night. That question, too, the investigator solved. Frank had told Sarah his work day ended at five, but the investigator found out he actually left work at four PM. When he travelled for business, training satellite companies, Sarah had no idea where he stayed or what he did after hours. He called her every night, but on his cell phone and there was no reason to suspect anything.

Frank was a quiet, unassuming guy and it wouldn't occur to any of their friends or family that he might have this secret life of pornography and being "serviced" by prostitutes. How could that have gone on for 16 years unseen was the question and so Sarah was labelled stupid for being unaware of his secret life and her financial losses. The fact of the matter was that Sarah was traumatized and moving forward in in a state of survival, and thus was unaware of the healing that needed to take place on her journey to wholeness.

We have a team on this side of the veil, who will support her, love her unconditionally and guide her out of this chaos to a place where eventually she will see this a gift. At this time, though Sarah was blaming herself since the circumstances were similar to those of her first failed marriage. She constantly berated herself for repeating the same mistakes even though they were glaring. Her penchant for judging herself was exacerbated by the lawyer's suggestion that Sarah should keep the information to herself. "Women have died for less, and when he finds out you have created another bank account and he will never see your money again, he will explode."

Frank was making plans to leave, to leave physically and leave all the debt behind on Sarah's shoulders. He also took to making strange loud noises in the night to scare Sarah and intimidate her into being acquiescent. Fortunately, it had a reverse effect and Sarah in her own quiet way had gone to war. As her spirit guides, we had to warn her of the temptation to gloat over knowing more about his actions than he ever might suspect that she knew. We also had to guide her in the right use of her time and energy when it came to revenge. Sarah would have startling dreams of how she would get revenge and Frank would receive his just desserts. That took some time and thoughtfulness on our part to convince her that the best revenge is to do well despite the huge obstacles that loomed ahead.

It took three years after Sarah and her husband separated that she felt she could hold her head up, be proud of her accomplishments and have a degree of compassion for Frank. There were dark moments when there seemed no hope and the people she trusted proved unworthy of the precious gift given to those she loved. But Sarah discovered there was a better life ahead because she chose to live an enlightened life despite the temptation to sit in despair and self-pity. Having said that, she experienced times of wallowing in self-pity, the desire to seek revenge and periods of feeling "stuck". What is important is how long did she hold on to old hurts and wounds? How often did she wake up at 3 in the morning re-playing her tapes of events? It's all part of a grieving process on the loss of a part of how she expected her life to be.

Reflection:

Part of the journey to healing is how does one reach out for help and what does that look like for each individual. A crucial realization is, we need and require an interdependent community where one gives a hand up to another in a pay it forward kind of way. Quite often how we expect to receive help is not the way it comes. We still have to do the work, but it is comforting to know we are loved and supported in the process. A sense of humor goes a long way and it is amazing how one can find humor in the darkest of moments. Laughter can shift energy easily and effortlessly and is much healthier than eating a tub of Pralines and Cream ice cream. Focusing our energy on gratitude is often a talked-about concept. And the truth is, we can find something to be grateful for no matter what the circumstances.

Sarah made it a practice to journal daily a list of what she wanted to accomplish and what she did. Listing five things for which she was grateful in the morning and again, the last thing she did at night worked like magic. Expect miracles. As long as she expected them and watched for them, she found them. She believed the best was yet to come as her soul evolved with its own song.

When life is tossed upside down it heralds something better coming your way. Be patient and you will see, she was assured over and over again. Fifteen years later Sarah had created a beautiful life where her business thrived, she enjoyed a family built on love and respect, and constantly sought to evolve into the best possible version of herself.

She needed to work on receiving, but she had come a long way and I was needed elsewhere. Sarah didn't notice for a while that I had moved on to assist another soul finding itself in a similar situation. Eventually she did and she called me in to her meditation and I willingly complied. She asked me where I had been and that she couldn't navigate life's curve balls without my assistance. I assured her she had the necessary courage and resilience to do just that and I was needed elsewhere. She agreed that I may be correct and I assured her I would return if she should need my guidance. She understood she had a whole new team of spirit guides that would guide her in this new phase of her life. To this day she tells others because she listened and followed our direction she does not regret anything she did or said during that time she was forced to look at how she was living life. And by making those changes she could live in her integrity and walk her talk. It is nice to be appreciated, but I was just doing my job.

And so it goes.

Reflection:

The learning from Sarah's perspective is to be able to step outside of your ego self and see yourself as an observer, especially during the trauma. Sarah sometimes wondered how this possibly could be a gift when her life was crashing down around her ears. She consistently received messages that a new and better life was just around the corner and that she would have to have faith. Her question was, how could she have faith when she could be penniless and living out of her car the next day?

There followed a host of synchronistic events that hadn't even occurred to her. She understood that once she was specific about what she wanted and needed, the possibility of finding solutions to these insurmountable problems was there, at least in her mind. Once she navigated a new healthier path, the gifts were abundant, and she started to see the light at the end of the tunnel and it wasn't a freight train! She tentatively reached out for help when it was desperately needed and it was there. She demonstrated to us on the other side that she knew the true meaning of surrender. It had nothing to do with throwing her hands up in the air and giving up her ability to manage the course her life was taking. She understood that once she was specific about what she wanted and created an action plan, all she had to do was take that baby step and let the Universe do its job. The Universe had a far better plan than what Sarah could ever conjure up by herself. How could she possibly know what it might look like if she had never witnessed or experienced it before? She learned to face those fears with core wounds exposed and raw and she did become fearless. Her next step was to move from fearlessness to courage, putting faith as the foremost priority toward true authenticity.

13
Let There Be Light

"Life can only be understood backwards; but it must be lived forwards."

—Soren Kierkegaard

Reflection:

The question is, what is your soul purpose? Is it the same for every life time and we just tweak it with every life evolution? We are here on earth to serve, but what does that mean? Do we serve ourselves in the pursuit of happiness or is our happiness dependent on the level we serve others?

With this burning question in mind, the quest became: at what point and in what lifetime did I understand and know without a doubt how I was supposed to serve others?

The deep cave was in darkness except for the flickering flame of the fire to warm the dampness. There was a sound of a hacking cough from further beyond where the ill and infirm were held in quarantine until the contagious aspect of the illness disappeared. I hoped I could have one night of blissful sleep, but that was a rarity. I was constantly summoned to someone's bedside either to administer a cold cloth, a poultice, or just hold a hand. I was a gifted shaman of the tribe and the tribe looked to me for healing on many levels. My sole purpose was to care for my fellow clansmen and train the young ones now growing into the role. This gift had been handed down through the generations and I was informed as a young child that I had a definite responsibility for life's expression and there was no turning back.

As I lay on my pallet I wondered what my life would have been had I grown up as one of the other children, making friends and creating havoc as they all did at one point of their growth. It was part of how they developed their identity, what was important to them and what made them sit up and take notice. That hadn't been my experience as I rose in the ranks of childhood, adolescence, and adulthood. While my path was very clear from birth, I never faltered from my perceived responsibility. The youth who might have been my girlfriends saw me as someone who thought she was better than everyone else. Nothing was further from the truth but perspectives are their reality and I couldn't explain why I preferred my solitude and favored my meanderings outside the cave as I deepened my connection with Spirit. Rather than intrigue my cohorts, my mystique irritated them and they looked for ways to demean and belittle me in front of others. I was poignantly aware of my unseen support and encouragement, but they did not serve to protect me in the living world. I often saw, felt, and heard images, colors, and textures that others couldn't and they supplied the knowledge and skills needed to care for the clan. They were my real friends, but that only added to others viewing me as an oddity.

In my younger years, my credibility with my contemporaries was of utmost importance.

As I grew older and wiser, I didn't look for it as was something to be acquired. It was something I was, rather than something to be acquired. And as the years passed it wasn't as entertaining to use me as the brunt of a prank or a joke and most clansmen accepted and revered me for who I was, the Shaman.

My hair attained a silvery blue hue and I wore it in a braid over my shoulder. My body was lean and well-muscled from many trips outside the caves to gather my inventory of herbs and medicines. My feet were callused from years of walking barefoot in the underbrush and stones of the creek bed. I never did take a mate, but had several connections reaffirming my divine feminine.

I had made my commitment to the village and they were my family. It will soon be time to select the next in line. I had already designated the little one who should be trained to take my place, and I only hoped she would take on her responsibility with the same fervor I had. This little one was high-spirited and would be a challenge to manage her spirit for the greater good without breaking her purity of heart. I realized she suspected she had been chosen when she was found crouching behind a rock eavesdropping on a meeting of the elders.

She must have overheard one elder say, "She's too high-spirited. She needs more years of maturity." Another said, "She doesn't listen and that above all is important." I nodded my head in sympathy, thinking, those were the very qualities that will make her a stellar healer rather than a mediocre one. She has the gift of clear sight from her heart and has a natural propensity to mix different herbs for a specific purpose. I wondered what was going through her head hiding behind that rock as she listened to what was being said about her. Poor dear, but she will have to get used to the scrutiny. That will just be a part of her life and she will have to grow a thick skin.

The next day the Little One burst into the space and demanded an audience with the elders to defend her honor. An attempt was made at straightening the curve of the Little One's lips as she remembered herself at that age. Her advice was to let it go and be the change the elders wanted to see in her. Her response was a loud harrumph as she strode out of her space with her short legs. Oddly enough given her expression of derision I expected her to become even more rebellious. But she must have at least given the advice consideration because she was the epitome of those attributes the elders discussed on a proposed initiate. I knew I had chosen well and she would be a mighty shaman, perhaps even more powerful than I am.

The months and years passed and the Little One was no longer little, but a tall, lithe, willowy woman with eyes of piercing blue. She knew who she was, she knew her purpose, and was now ready to take a leadership role. A feast was arranged and the drums were heard inviting other clans to the ceremony of leadership. Special dishes were prepared and everyone in the clan had a task in preparation for this gala event. The Little One was sequestered for a week in meditation and learning the vows and their import for her new position in the clan. She stayed with me that week as readied herself in body, mind, and spirit. It was our special time for the transfer of the mantle to another and I was proud to my very core. This one will be praiseworthy in all facets of her duty!

The evening finally arrived as I led the Initiate, the clansmen, and visitors outside the cave on the narrow path leading up the side of the mountain. Spirit would begin the initiation as the sun set and we were ready to receive. We took our ascribed places and looked to the heavens. As the sun teetered on the edge of the adjoining mountain, a shaft of light found its way to the initiate who had arms and hands outstretched. The pillar of light divided into three beams, infusing light in both her hands and the crown of her head. The halo appearing briefly over my head moved over and above the initiate's head. Finally, there was a voice heard by all standing by which pronounced, "And she will be called Anya."

www.ingramcontent.com/pod-product-compliance
Lightning Source LLC
Chambersburg PA
CBHW070154080526
44586CB00015B/1986